Queen of Egypt

Written by Frances Bacon
Illustrated by Nilesh Mistry

Egypt

Contents

Who Was Cleopatra?

Cleopatra was the last queen of Egypt. She ruled Egypt over 2,000 years ago—from 51 B.C. to 30 B.C. Although Cleopatra lived so long ago, she is one of the most famous women in history. Ancient writings tell us that Cleopatra was charming, intelligent, and ambitious. She is remembered not only for her own power but also for the influence that she had over the two most powerful men in the world at that time—Julius Caesar and Mark Antony.

In Cleopatra's time, Egypt was an important country, but it lived in the shadow of mighty Rome. Cleopatra was desperate to keep Egypt independent of Roman rule. In the end, Rome was too powerful to hold back, but Cleopatra's story lives on.

about 70 B.C.

Cleopatra is born in Alexandria, Egypt.

51 B.C.

Cleopatra becomes Queen of Egypt.

48 B.C.

Cleopatra is driven out of Egypt. She returns in secret and meets Julius Caesar.

about 46 B.C.

Cleopatra goes to Rome with Julius Caesar and their son, Caesarian.

Setting the Scene

Ancient Egypt

In 332 B.C., the Macedonian king, Alexander the Great, conquered Egypt and founded the city of Alexandria. When Alexander died, Ptolemy (*TAHL uh mee*), one of his generals, made himself king of Egypt. The Ptolemys (Cleopatra's family) ruled Egypt for 300 years, and Alexandria became an important center of learning and the arts. Its library was the largest in the world.

In Cleopatra's time, Egypt (red) was in a region that was largely ruled by Rome (orange).

Rome
Actium
Tarsus
Mediterranean Sea
SYRIA
Alexandria
EGYPT

44 B.C.	41 B.C.	32 B.C.	30 B.C.
Julius Caesar dies. Cleopatra and Caesarian return to Egypt.	Cleopatra meets Mark Antony in Tarsus (now in Turkey). They fall in love.	Octavian, a Roman leader, declares war on Egypt. Mark Antony fights for Cleopatra.	Cleopatra and Mark Antony die. Egypt comes under Roman rule.

Princess Cleopatra

54 B.C.

*Princess Cleopatra listened carefully to the whisperings of
the servants. She was the only member of the royal family
who spoke Egyptian—the language of the people. She knew
that the servants' gossip was true: her father was a bad ruler.
Egypt was becoming poorer and poorer, and the people
were angry because of Ptolemy XII's high taxes.
It was only support from the rulers in Rome that kept
the king in power. Cleopatra loved her father, but
she also loved Egypt. She longed to make Egypt
as powerful as it had been in the ancient time
of the pharaohs. For now, however, all she
could do was listen, study, and learn.*

pharaoh an Egyptian ruler from ancient times

Cleopatra was one of six children born to King Ptolemy XII. She grew up in Alexandria, in a large, luxurious palace with many servants. Tutors taught her math, Greek literature, philosophy, and public speaking. She was the most gifted of the children and is said to have spoken eight languages—the rest of her family spoke only Greek.

The royal family was not a happy one. The children were rivals for the throne, and life was political and dangerous. Cleopatra's desire to rule kept her going, but she knew that she had enemies.

Today, Alexandria is a busy city on Egypt's Mediterranean coast.

Queen of Egypt

Cleopatra was worried. Being queen of Egypt did not make her safe. She knew that her brother, Ptolemy XIII, who ruled beside her, was trying to send her out of Egypt. His advisers felt that Cleopatra had too much power. They were right to be concerned. Cleopatra was desperate to rule on her own. Only then could she make Egypt a great nation again.

For the past three years, Cleopatra and Ptolemy XIII had fought each other for control. Finally, Cleopatra's worst fears were coming true. Ptolemy XIII's supporters had become too strong to ignore. Cleopatra knew she must flee to Syria or risk losing her life.

Cleopatra's father died in 51 B.C. In his will, he named Cleopatra, who was 19, and her brother Ptolemy XIII, who was only 10, as his successors. The throne had been expected to go to Ptolemy XIII alone, but the old king knew how clever Cleopatra was, so he had declared that the brother and sister should rule together.

Ptolemy XIII's advisers did not like Cleopatra. Finally, they forced her to flee to Syria, where she gathered an army and made plans to fight back. Cleopatra knew she had to be cunning. Her brother had threatened to have her killed if she returned.

This ancient coin shows Cleopatra in profile. While lacking great beauty, she was known for her charm and wit.

successor a person who becomes a ruler when another ruler dies

9

A Surprise for Caesar

Cleopatra heard the news—Julius Caesar, one of the most powerful men in Rome, was visiting Egypt. She thought that if she could meet him, she could persuade him to help her. First, however, she had to get back into Egypt and past her brother's guards. Cleopatra made a plan.

In secret, she sailed across the Mediterranean Sea. Then, hidden by the dark of night, she climbed into a small boat and sailed into Alexandria. Finally, she rolled herself in a blanket, and a servant carried her past the guards and into the palace. Caesar was astonished when the queen of Egypt rolled out of the blanket placed at his feet!

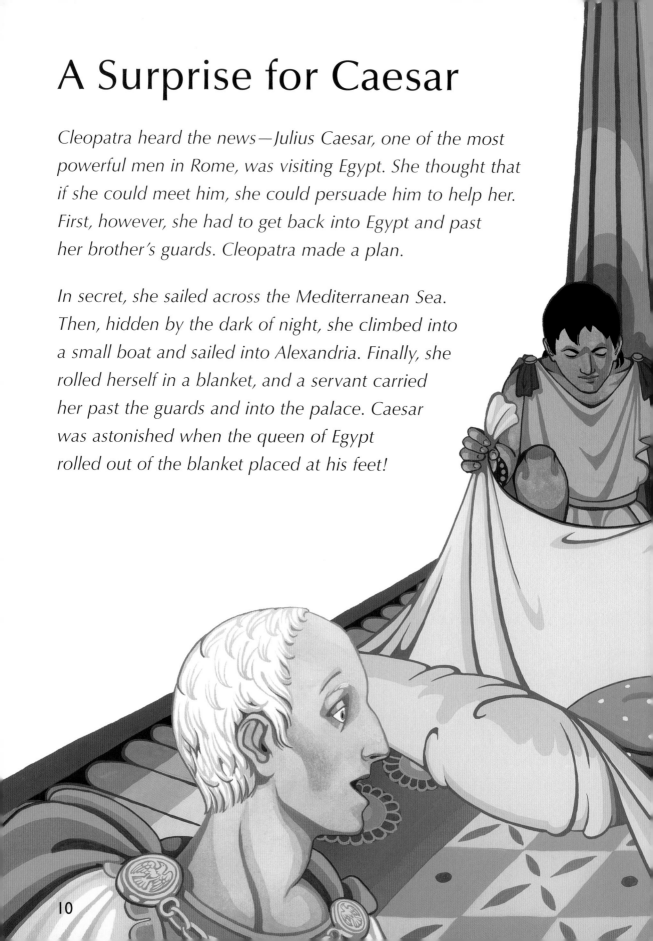

Cleopatra *"is a person to be wondered at ... whom dreamers find always at the end of their dreams."*
—Theophile Gautier, French poet

While Cleopatra had been gathering supporters in Syria, fighting had broken out in the Roman Empire between two generals, Julius Caesar and Pompey. Caesar went to Egypt to fight Pompey, but when he got there, he found that Pompey was already dead—he had been killed by his own soldiers!

Instead, Caesar met the dazzling Cleopatra. Although Caesar was 52 and Cleopatra was just 22, they had much in common. They were both powerful, ambitious, and intelligent. It wasn't long before Caesar and Cleopatra were in love.

Julius Caesar was a powerful leader who oversaw the expansion of the Roman Empire.

Roman Empire   a group of countries under Roman rule

11

Cruising the Nile

47 B.C.

Crowds of excited people lined the banks of the River Nile to see Queen Cleopatra and Julius Caesar sail past on the royal barge. Cleopatra was proudly showing Caesar her country. For several weeks, they sailed upriver, gliding past ancient temples and palaces. Caesar was impressed with what he saw. He was also impressed with the way the Egyptian people treated Cleopatra as if she were a goddess. Caesar was the most important man in the Roman Empire. If he were to marry Cleopatra, together they would rule most of the known world.

Cleopatra and Caesar tried to bring peace to Egypt, but Ptolemy XIII's army constantly attacked them. After six months, Caesar ordered his army to fight back. Ptolemy XIII tried to escape in a small boat, but it capsized, and the 15-year-old king drowned. Once more, Cleopatra was crowned queen of Egypt. This time, her youngest brother, 12-year-old Ptolemy XIV, was at her side.

With Ptolemy XIII dead, Cleopatra was free to rule Egypt her way. Julius Caesar stayed with her for a year, and they had a son, named Caesarian. Meanwhile, in Rome, Caesar's generals feared that the power of his enemies was growing. They urged Caesar to return to Rome.

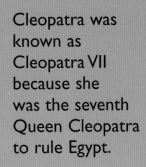

Cleopatra was known as Cleopatra VII because she was the seventh Queen Cleopatra to rule Egypt.

The Best-Laid Plans

Cleopatra loved living in Rome. She, along with Caesarian and Ptolemy XIV, had been living with Caesar for two years now. Her plan to get the Roman government to make a new treaty of friendship with Egypt had gone well. With Caesar's support, the treaty had been passed quickly and easily. Now Egypt was safe, and Caesar was well on his way to becoming the king of Rome. Cleopatra looked up from her reading as a messenger rushed into the room.

"Your highness, the mighty Caesar has been stabbed by his enemies. Caesar is dead!" The messenger bowed and left, leaving the grief-stricken and vulnerable Egyptian queen behind.

treaty an agreement between two or more groups

In 47 B.C., Caesar's generals had finally managed to get him to leave Egypt—and Cleopatra. However, it wasn't long before Cleopatra and her family joined Caesar in Rome. The pair entertained famous thinkers, politicians, and other important people in Caesar's villa on the banks of the River Tiber. While some politicians supported Caesar and Cleopatra, others were nervous about the ambitious pair.

On March 15, 44 B.C., Caesar's enemies stabbed him at the Roman forum. With Caesar gone, Cleopatra knew that she, too, was in danger, so she and her family returned to Egypt.

Today, thousands of people visit the ruins of the ancient forum in Rome, Italy, every year.

forum a public space used for business and politics

Antony and Cleopatra

41 B.C.

Power in Rome was now shared among three men. One of them was the handsome Mark Antony. He needed Cleopatra's help to remain in power, so he sent for her. Cleopatra, however, refused to be ordered around. She was a queen, and she demanded respect. Antony sent more messages, which Cleopatra also ignored. Then, finally, she agreed to meet him.

When Mark Antony at last met Cleopatra, he was stunned. She was dressed magnificently as Aphrodite, the Greek goddess of love. He soon discovered, however, that Cleopatra was a woman who could bargain as well as any man.

Like Caesar before him, Mark Antony was soon in love with Cleopatra. Although their relationship was based on true feelings, it also had political benefits for them both. Cleopatra had great wealth, which Mark Antony needed in his battle for power in Rome. In return, Antony could offer Egypt protection from a Roman invasion. As the love grew between Antony and Cleopatra, so too did their political power.

Mark Antony had been an officer under Julius Caesar. He hoped to one day be sole ruler of Rome.

The Rise of Egypt

The crowd watching the great ceremony thought that their leaders looked more than human. Cleopatra and Antony were dressed as gods and sat on thrones of solid gold. Cleopatra smiled majestically as Antony gave her large parts of the eastern territories of the Roman Empire. Most of these lands had once belonged to Egypt, and Cleopatra finally had them back. For years, her goal had been to rebuild the Egyptian Empire, and now she seemed to be achieving it.

Cleopatra and Antony's three children also received Roman lands. Then, in a brave move, Antony declared Caesarian "King of Kings" and Caesar's heir to the Roman Empire.

Back in Rome, Octavian, Caesar's stepson and Antony's main rival, was furious. Octavian believed that he, not Caesarian, should be Caesar's heir. He told the Roman government that Cleopatra had Antony under her control. He accused Antony of preferring Alexandria to Rome and of behaving as if he were a king. The Romans agreed that Antony should not be giving parts of the Empire to a foreign queen.

In 32 B.C., Octavian declared war on Cleopatra. He knew that Antony was too important to attack directly, but he also knew that Antony would do anything to protect his beloved Egyptian queen.

A carving of Cleopatra and her son Caesarian at a temple in Dendera, Egypt

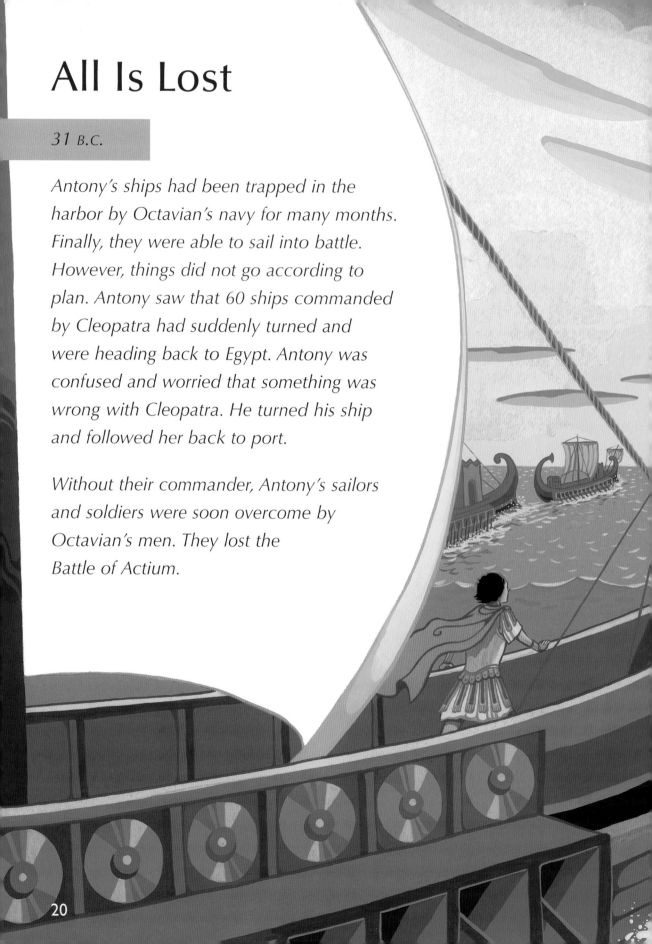

All Is Lost

Antony's ships had been trapped in the harbor by Octavian's navy for many months. Finally, they were able to sail into battle. However, things did not go according to plan. Antony saw that 60 ships commanded by Cleopatra had suddenly turned and were heading back to Egypt. Antony was confused and worried that something was wrong with Cleopatra. He turned his ship and followed her back to port.

Without their commander, Antony's sailors and soldiers were soon overcome by Octavian's men. They lost the Battle of Actium.

Historians have argued for years about why Cleopatra ordered her ships to leave the Battle of Actium. Some say that she was scared and that she betrayed Antony for her own safety. However, Cleopatra was famous for her strong will and her courage. Perhaps she was trying to save Egypt's treasure, which was in the hold of her ship. Whatever the reason, it was the beginning of the end for both Cleopatra and Antony.

Cleopatra died shortly afterward. Historians believe that she took her own life. Octavian's army captured Egypt, and it became part of the Roman Empire. Cleopatra did, however, get her final wish—she and Antony were buried in the same tomb.

This painting, *The Battle of Actium*, was painted by Italian artist Neroccio de' Landi in the 15th century.

A Woman of Influence

Cleopatra ruled Egypt for 22 years. Her reputation as an intelligent, ambitious ruler has lasted for more than 2,000 years. She was an incredibly powerful leader in a time when women were considered second to men and queens were second to kings. Two of the greatest men in the world loved her, and many more feared her.

The Romans felt threatened by Cleopatra and called her the "serpent of the Nile." The Egyptians, however, continued to worship her long after her death. Despite the fact that Egypt did, in the end, become part of the Roman Empire, Cleopatra was undoubtedly one of the greatest leaders ever to rule Egypt.

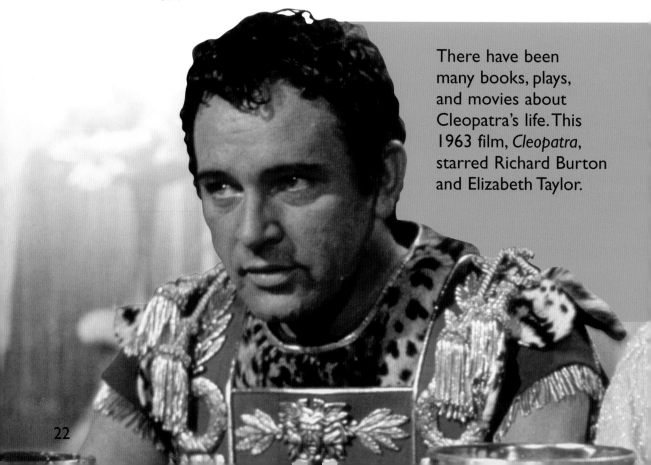

There have been many books, plays, and movies about Cleopatra's life. This 1963 film, *Cleopatra*, starred Richard Burton and Elizabeth Taylor.